The Confident DIY Painter

How to Use General Finishes Paint to Get a Professional, Durable Finish for Your Kitchen and Bathroom Cabinets

Rachel Elise Trimble

The Confident DIY Painter

Printed by:
90-Minute Books
302 Martinique Drive
Winter Haven, FL 33884
www.90minutebooks.com

Copyright © 2016, Rachel Elise Trimble

Published in the United States of America

Book ID: 160718-00474

ISBN-13: 978-1945733130
ISBN-10: 1945733136:

For more information on 90-Minute Books including finding out how you can
publish your own lead generating book, visit www.90minutebooks.com or call
(863) 318-0464

Here's What's Inside…

Introduction

Kitchens are truly the heart of a home. I love working with clients who have the goal to make their current house one step closer to their perfect dream home, but don't have a huge budget to do so. Painting cabinets is an economical way to take a 1980s kitchen out of the sitcom era and erase the disappointing feeling that you cannot afford a magazine-worthy kitchen.

Painted cabinets done well can add thousands of dollars to the value of your home. On the flip side, if you take on this project and mess it up, you can instantly subtract many more thousands from your home's current value. The whole process can be overwhelming, and I'm here to show you that it doesn't need to be. There are a lot of people who would love to update their cabinets but have "analysis paralysis" and are too scared to begin because they don't have the confidence.

I'm here to change all that.

In our DIY classes at our studio in Phoenix, we have classes that detail our entire process, including everything from how to prep cabinets for paint, to the ins and outs of top coating with sealer. We recently had a couple take our class who had been contemplating painting their cabinets for a long time. They had done so much research about products, supplies, methods of applications, etc. They were stressed out just talking about finishing their kitchen remodel project, especially because they weren't experienced painters. However, hiring refinishers simply wasn't in their budget. They both signed up for our class and felt so much more confident after being walked through the process.

It's kind of like riding a bike: scary at first, a few bumps and bruises (kind of like finding a drip or overworking a top coat), but once you get in the groove, you realize how much freedom comes with a new skill. This couple was able to tackle their kitchen together and is so proud of their updated space. They love showing it off to friends and family who visit and who can't believe they didn't hire a professional.

We recently helped a couple that was ready to list their home for sale in a very competitive and saturated market. They wanted to make their home stand out and knew that by updating their kitchen prior to professional listing photos, they would increase the number of people who would make appointments to see it. By restyling their high-quality, but orangey, cabinets to a distressed, Antique White finish and going with a classic black kitchen island, their MLS listing stood out from the crowd. They had tons of traffic, and the house went under contract in just two weeks for more money than they expected.

Imagine what it will mean for you to have the updated kitchen and bathroom you always wanted, at a fraction of the cost?!

Enjoy the book!

I hope this book gives you the confidence to paint your own kitchen or bathroom cabinets, so you can enjoy your home more, or if you are selling it, make more money!

To Your Fabulous "New to You" Kitchen!

Rachel

Why Do a Lot of DIY Painters Lack Confidence?

Susan: This is Susan Austin, and I'm excited to be here with Rachel Elise Trimble. Rachel is going to be sharing with us her thoughts and ideas on how to use General Finishes paint to get a professional, durable finish for your kitchen and bathroom cabinets! Welcome, Rachel!

Rachel: Good morning, Susan. So glad to be here!

Susan: Why do you think more do-it-yourself painters lack confidence when it comes to painting their bathroom and kitchen cabinets?

Rachel: I love that question because I see it in the people who visit our shop all the time. They come in, and they're excited to take on their cabinets, but they lack the confidence to actually get started. The number one reason for this is that they are overwhelmed. There is so much information out there—on Pinterest, on YouTube, blogs—and a lot of the information is conflicting. There are so many different product choices, different ways to prep, and different ways to seal that it overwhelms them, and the result of that is they don't ever get started. A cabinet refinishing job is often the largest home-improvement job that these people will take on themselves, so they know that if they don't get it right, instead of adding tons of value to their homes, they could be instantly detracting value, so it's a little scary to them, and rightly so.

They're worried they're not going to get a durable finish. They're concerned about the colors that they choose.

They don't want to be too trendy. If they go with gray now, is that a bad choice if they decide to sell in three years? Are they really limiting themselves? There are a lot of choices to be made. Even simple things like, where do they get the supplies? There are so many brushes out there, where do they even start to pick the right one for what they want to accomplish? Where should they go? Do they go to the paint store, or do they go to their local hardware store? Do they order from Amazon? There is just so much information to sift through once you Google "painting cabinets." A lot of the people I speak with have taken on projects like painting their house walls, but painting cabinets is a totally different animal, and they're not really sure where to start. They get stuck trying to decide what products they're going to buy, what methods they're going to apply, and they don't know if they can do it by hand or if they have to invest in expensive equipment to get a professional finish?

Susan: Do you know of people who have messed up their cabinets, made a muck of it, and regretted taking it on?

Rachel: Unfortunately, yes. Several times a week we get a call from someone who said that they chose X, Y, Z product, and it didn't work right. They mess them up because sometimes they'll use an oil-based product, and in their rush to get them done, they don't let them dry long enough in between coats. So they end up with a sticky mess, or they'll use the wrong top coat. Then they've painted beautiful, white cabinets, and they start to turn yellow, which is very upsetting, as you can imagine.

Or perhaps they didn't spend the time to prep properly, and now they have peeling paint, so they'll call us and ask us what to do. Unfortunately, when this happens, it's not a happy answer for them.

Susan: All of those would be devastating if they happened to me.

Rachel: Yes, it's very frustrating when that happens, but hopefully with what they learn in this book or other classes I can point them to, they won't make the same mistakes.

How to Fall in Love with Your Home Again

Susan: If someone is able to take on a DIY project and paint by themselves, their kitchen or bathroom cabinets, what will it mean to them?

Rachel: What's really exciting to us is we work with a lot of first-time home buyers. They've saved and saved and planned their dream home. The reality of it is, their starter home doesn't really feel like a home; it feels more like a house because they don't have all the dream amenities they see in magazines and always thought they would get. Being able to paint your own cabinets means turning this house and this investment—the largest investment they've made to date in their lives—into a place that they feel proud of, into their home.

People don't want to spend so much time working and planning and paying mortgages to come home to a house that looks like it came right out of a 1980s sitcom. By painting their kitchens and bathrooms, they can really identify more with today's magazines and what's on trend and not have to go home every day to ugly, honey oak cabinets. There's really nothing like a sense of pride when you have accomplished something at this level. That's why we always encourage people to take before-and-after pictures. When you're in the thick of all this prepping and painting and DIY mess, sometimes at the end you don't realize what it looked like before. Another thing that's great is that they're adding value.

When they do it the right way, they're adding thousands of dollars of value to their home, so it's not just the way it makes them feel, but it's real, tangible value that they're adding by updating their space.

You know, a lot of people here in Arizona have peach flooring, and flooring is very, very costly to replace. Even if you did it yourself, it's very time-consuming to remove it. It's messy. You have to buy and lay new tile, so the best way to live with your flooring and not hate it so much is to draw attention away from it. Often, if you pick the right color for your cabinetry, your flooring will be a lot less noticeable, so that's another benefit.

You know, Susan, we work with a lot of people who haven't just bought their first home; they're looking to sell their home. When we speak with realtors, we find out that they can't even get people to come and see their listings that have outdated kitchens and bathrooms because nowadays you go online and look at an MLS listing before you're willing to decide, "Should I work all day and then go drive across town to see this house?" When a homeowner takes the time to paint their cabinets and then have professional pictures taken, it's already increasing the pool of potential customers for their home because kitchens and bathrooms sell homes. People will want to come and see their listing just because it looks updated, and they're not spending all that time calculating, "How much is this house going to cost me, once I move in, to get it up to today's standards?" It's really another benefit of taking that project on.

Susan: They'll draw from a better pool of buyers who are willing to pay more for an updated kitchen, I would imagine. Do you know how much value having updated cabinets adds to a home? Is there any way to guesstimate how much value is being added?

Rachel: There are two ways to look at it. A typical job for my company in Arizona would be, let's say $3,500 to professionally refinish a kitchen of a 3,000-square-foot home. To have that refaced with new veneer and new doors, that's about $10,000 to $12,000, and if you gutted your kitchen, it's at least $25,000 to $40,000 to start all over. Just by doing it yourself, you're already adding thousands of dollars of value and taking away $3,500 of expenses. But when we're talking about selling your home, it is quantifiable because let's say you list your house at $250,000, and there's no bites because you have the honey oak, graham-cracker-looking cabinets, and a buyer who's looking at a $250,000 home won't necessarily have another $4,000 in cash, or $10,000, or even $30,000 to put into that home to update it. If you do the cabinets, you can list your house higher than the comps in the neighborhood that don't have updates. Not only will you be able to list your house higher, you're going to attract more potential buyers because it is updated.

What do those numbers mean? It depends on every neighborhood and every price point, but I've been told by realtors that painting your cabinets means at least $10,000 to the value of your home because kitchens and bathrooms sell homes.

You can start with a higher listing price number than your neighbors with outdated kitchens and bathrooms can. Plus, it will sell faster, and that usually means more dollars in your pocket too.

Susan: I love it. I think everyone should at least look into this because, in the end, even if you do it for them, it's not that much money. It may be time—we're going to get into that in a moment—but I think, of all the people who are putting up with a kitchen they don't love but they just don't have the $20,000 to remove the cabinets and put a whole new kitchen in, this is a fantastic alternative to that.

Rachel: Right and it's not just the money, either. It's the time. We have pets, we have families, we have jobs, all sorts of stuff, so it's really a commitment to have everything replaced, but if you could do this with water-based products, you can do it in your home and don't need a whole crazy station taking over your house to spray it. You're really taking the displacement factor out of a home remodeling project, at that magnitude.

The 6 Things Every DIY Painter Needs to Know

Susan: Let's talk about what they need to know to paint beautiful, durable cabinets, Rachel. Walk us through the six things every do-it-yourself painter needs to know to create beautiful, durable cabinets.

Rachel: The first thing they should understand is that by painting their cabinets themselves they can save thousands of dollars and at the same time add thousands of dollars to the value of their home. Kitchens and bathrooms are typically the heart of the home so updated kitchens and bathrooms sell homes.

The second point they need to know is to start small and go bigger over time. I often tell people, "Get your toe wet first." Do your bathroom first. Live with it for a little bit. See how good that feels. See if you can start walking down to get your coffee in the morning and picture your kitchen differently. You don't have to take on a huge project for your first attempt at a DIY painting. Then you can ease into these types of projects like an entire kitchen.

The next thing people need to understand is that all paint is not created equal. It's important to have the right kind of paint on your cabinets. Paint has come a long way over the years. Today, you don't need to use oil, but latex isn't the answer either. When you visit the craft or paint store, you will find a huge variety of specialty paints that have been formulated for different uses and applications on an array of surfaces. This can definitely be overwhelming and daunting to the average homeowner when it comes to selecting the appropriate paint for your DIY cabinet project.

I personally love the General Finishes milk paint because it's actually a highly engineered acrylic-based paint that is perfect for adhering to wood and other substrate surfaces.

Another thing to consider is what equipment is needed for your DIY cabinet painting project. With the process we use in my shop in Arizona, it is not necessary to use expensive equipment to have beautiful results. You just need to know the right supplies to have on hand to make the job as simple as possible. There are hundreds of sprayers on the market. Do you use that really inexpensive sprayer that's $99, or do you go out and buy a professional one that's a lot more, or do you even need to go the sprayer route? We have sprayed before, but I feel that we get a beautiful finish by using a hand-roller as well as a few brushes for the application of paint. There is no need to go out and buy an expensive sprayer and spend the time and the money to learn how to use complicated equipment. There's plenty of ways to complete your project by hand to get beautiful results.

One of the most important steps in the process is knowing how to prep your cabinets for paint. If you skimp on this step, you're going to be very sorry, and you will probably be one of the people who call during the week, telling us how upset you are.

We get calls from people, telling us their neighbor didn't sand them and wondering why they have to. I say, "You can do whatever you want, but if you want a professional finish, yes, prep—and that means lightly sanding—is definitely the most important part."

With General Finishes products, you don't need to use oil-based paints, like old-school people might tell you. The water-based paints have come so far. They're low VOC, they're pet- and child-friendly, and they're easier to use because of the way that they're engineered, which makes DIY projects so much easier than they used to be.

Susan: Talk to us about colors. It's so overwhelming, Rachel, to try to come up with a color because as you hinted earlier, if you screw this part up, I don't care how good it looks, if it's not the right color for your house, it's going to stand out in a bad way. Help!

Rachel: Exactly. Talking about not having confidence in your cabinets, I meet people all the time who say, "I'm not a designer. I'm not good with color. I'm not stylish. I don't know what to do." That's why I like the General Finishes palette: It's quite simplified, in general, because they have a white called Snow White and an off-white called Antique White. There are some other cream colors, too, but I always have thought picking white is the hardest thing to do. With their color palette, their Snow White is perfect if you have white and gray counter-tops, and your house can handle the white-white. If not, they have the Antique White color, which is slightly off-white.

If you're transitioning from a 1980s home or a Tuscan-themed home, then you're going to have a lot of warm tones in your house, and so if you choose the Antique White, it's basically like painting your cabinets white, but it's not going to have that stark contrast, and it's going to be a prettier color for your home.

I really think that they've taken the guesswork out of the colors with their color palette, but if there's something that you have to have or you have to match something else, your designer picked it, your best friend did it, and you have to do it, then you can contact your General Finishes retailer, and they can have the milk paint actually tinted to the exact color that you want. The other thing with regard to General Finishes products, which we use, is that they have a High Performance Top Coat that is easy to use. Even professionals don't love to apply top coat because it looks like you're messing up your perfectly painted cabinets. That's where so many cabinet jobs go wrong. If you use the wrong top coat, you're going to get streaks in it, and it can make your paint turn yellow. They have come up with a product that is just extremely durable, paired with their paint. It will give you a professional look, it's easy to apply, and it totally won't yellow.

We tell people, "Don't be scared. It's just paint. It can be sanded down. You can fix it." Honestly, if you spend the time to paint your cabinets, you're going to wonder, when you look at your before pictures, why you spent such a long time living the way you did before.

Susan: Interesting!

Even if they do pick a color they're not in love with, when they're all said and done, you're saying that, worst-case scenario, they can just start over?

Rachel: Well, it's just paint, but I would definitely say you wouldn't want the heartache of doing the whole thing and re-installing and top-coating because then you're starting completely over.

What you can do—and what I teach in my class—is to get your learning curve over on the back of the cabinet. If you're contemplating between colors, paint a couple of the cabinet backs, hold them up, and see which one works the best in your space.

That's why when DIYers turn to General Finishes paint, there are only several colors of white and cream, and it just feels very obvious, once it's in your space, to see which one looks better with your counter-tops and floors. It really takes a lot of analysis paralysis out of it, by not having 50 shades of white to choose from.

Susan: That's a nightmare. I think less is more, in some cases. General Finishes has already done the heavy lifting and picked paint that looks great in today's kitchens. That is very reassuring.

Rachel: Exactly. If you go to **www.GeneralFinishes.com**, they actually have showcases of different kitchens, with before and after pictures, in their color, so you can find a kitchen that has some of your counter-tops and perhaps your flooring and see it, before and after. It is always nice to have a reference like that. Also, at **www.restylejunkie.com**, we're always sharing our work on Instagram and Facebook, so you can see what colors are popular and see a lot of before-and-after pictures there as well.

Susan: Very good. Talk to us about some of the other types of paints that are on the market, in case people are unsure if General Finishes is the way to go. How do they make that kind of decision?

Rachel: One big thing to keep in mind is that some paints look better only sprayed.

I feel that General Finishes looks good sprayed or hand-rolled, so that's significant. If you want a professional finish when using the applied by hand method, then General Finishes is the way to go. Some different paints are oil-based, and you might not want that paint smell in your house while you're doing it. Also, oil-based paints take a lot longer to dry, and some of the hybrid paints do as well. By using a water-based paint, the dry times are certainly a lot faster, and it accelerates the speed of your project and the dry times.

Susan: By how much?

Rachel: A popular product out there says 16 hours between coats, so you're only really getting 1 coat, and then the next day, you have to flip it. In the desert here in Phoenix, we can put on another coat within an hour or two of painting.

Susan: Oh, wow, that's quite a difference.

Rachel: Dry times are going to depend on how much humidity and the weather where you are located, but definitely a couple hours, usually no more than four hours. With General Finishes milk paint; you can get more done at once, specifically with the top coat.

There's another user-friendly DIY type of paint out there that is typically finished with wax. Personally, I think that's beautiful and great for a piece of furniture that's not in a high-use area. If you want to have durable, professional looking cabinets, you need a paint that's sticks to almost everything.

Water-based milk paint, which is rated interior and exterior grade, paired with High Performance top coat is going to give you that durability you want, but if you go ahead and top your kitchen cabinets with wax, that's not a permanent solution.

The wax is going to have to be redone, sometimes as often as yearly. It also doesn't give you the scrubability of the High Performance top coat that General Finishes does. We don't use wax in professional jobs because of the durability. Perhaps in a powder room or something like that you can get away with it, but if you're looking for something that's going to be extremely durable and can stand up to the wear-and-tear of a kitchen, you definitely want to choose a paint that's made for wood and is sealed as good as with that top coat.

Susan: Can you paint over a wax-based paint?

Rachel: You actually can't, and that's a big thing too. You have to sand it all the way down, so if you put on some sort of paint where you put wax over it, you decide to change it or need to touch it up, or it gets messed up, you're sanding that whole thing down all the way to get the wax off because it won't be able to accept other paint after that. That's really something to consider. Wax is kind of a permanent choice when you go there, and it won't last as long.

Susan: Let's talk a little bit more in-depth about the prepping because I know this is a big concern for a lot of people.

We do see YouTube tutorials where they just take the cabinet off and paint it without prepping. How much of a difference does the sanding make?

Rachel: It makes all the difference in the world. Have you ever heard your mother say, "A job worth doing is a job worth doing right? It's the same thing here.

Your finish is only as good as what you're putting it on, so you could put it on beautifully, you could have no brush strokes and do a beautiful job, but if you're not giving it something to stick to, it's going to be a problem. You know those bumper things, the little felt or plastic things that are on the corners that keep your cabinets from hitting the frame?

If you decide it's too much work to take those off properly when you're cleaning, and you don't get that entire residue off, that will give your new paint job a place to lift up, so even if you do a great job, you could be exposing your cabinets to an easy way to show wear-and-tear. You really want to take the time beforehand to clean your cabinets. The entire process will go faster if you take the time in the beginning to do things properly. Our cabinets are exposed to so many oils and greases from cooking to lotions on our hands. Those really have to come off in order to give paint a nice place to adhere. Painting cabinets is not rocket science, but it is laborious, and it does take some time and some patience, but you get what you put into it.

The Common Mistakes DIY Painters Make When Painting Their Cabinets

Susan: I think it would be really helpful if you could walk us through some of the mistakes you've seen do-it-yourselfers make. I know I learn really well from people who have messed something up, so I know what to be on the lookout for.

Rachel: One of the biggest mistakes, of course, is rushing through it and skimping on the prep that we just spoke about. I mean, this is not the time to rush. It's not a race. Nobody's timing you, so don't skimp on the prep work. It's just not worth it. It's not worth it to go through all the other steps if you're going to skimp on the prep. Buying paint because it's cheap is another mistake. Sometimes you don't have to buy designer simply because it's more expensive, but General Finishes milk paints are highly engineered paints that are made for wood surfaces and other surfaces that aren't walls. A little bit goes a long way with it, but you have to look at it as an investment in some of the products that you're buying. Cheap paint is just that. It is cheap paint, and it will show.

We get this one a lot, too: They use a product because they already have it on hand. Maybe they've prepped everything right. They've used the right type of paint, and then they had a top coat that they've had sitting in their garage for five years because they didn't want to invest more. This is a bad idea. Things in your garage, because of the heat and cold, don't do well over time. I promise you that it will look different on your cabinets. Just because you have it on hand doesn't mean you need to use it, especially on your cabinets.

Another mistake we see is not applying the paint or top coat correctly. If you put on paint too thin, that's never a problem because you can keep adding coats to it. However, if you put it on too thick and overwork it, it's easy enough to fix, but it is kind of a pain. After you apply General Finishes milk paint or top coat you need to just walk away, and let it do its evening out thing. It's incredible how beautifully it flows. You don't have to go over it ten times to make it perfect and that's what makes it an excellent choice for both professionals and DIYers.

When you're painting your cabinets, weather sensitivity comes into play. The paint does better in 70-degree humidity and temperature, which, here in the desert, isn't exactly easy to achieve. The Southwest's 76 degrees is usually everyone else's 70 degrees. You don't want to do your cabinets when it's too hot. Your paint will dry too quickly before it can even out. Likewise, if it's too cold, your paint isn't going to flow out either. Paint your cabinets in an environment where you can control the temperature, and you can also control the amount of debris floating around as well. If you're going to do this in your backyard, and it's October, with the leaves falling off your tree, you want to make sure that they're not going into your cabinet. We've had people tell us, "Hey, I painted these outside and have leaves and other little insects in my paint." That's going to require some sandpaper and time to fix. Avoid this by doing this in the right environment.

It's so disappointing to have beautiful white cabinets and put on a top coat that's going to yellow over time. Choosing the right top coat for your cabinets is critical.

You can also keep it simple. You really don't have to overachieve the first time around. You don't have to add glaze to make them look beautiful.

You're already updating them so much, so you don't have to take on something that, artistically, is out of your comfort zone.

The last mistake is one of our troubleshooting things, and this scares people, too. So many products say you don't need to sand or prime. Technically, yes. The paint will go on if you don't sand or prime, but we tell our DIY clients that there are tannins in wood, and specific cabinets should be primed beforehand to block any of the wood tannins coming through, so you don't mess up your light paint job. Just because it doesn't say to, if you want a professional finish, then oftentimes it's much better to use a primer first.

If your paint is peeling, this can be a big problem. Typically, we try and find out where it went wrong. Why are they not getting a professional finish? Sometimes their missteps can be attributed to not priming, and perhaps they have some bleed-through, or they didn't prep it properly, like we talked about with the sticky bumper thing, so the paint is lifting. Or they didn't take the time to clean everything off, or they've used an old-school, oil-based top coat, and it's yellowing and making their white cabinets look awful. Those are the top three things that we hear often. Some of them are not too hard to fix, but a lot of them require you to do them again. You have to sand it down and basically start the process over. You might not have to go back to the raw, but you've got to make sure that your cabinets are cleaned and you're using the right top coat.

Honestly, the things people are most scared of are brush strokes and drips.

I promise you, with this General Finishes milk paint, those are not the calls we're getting. It evens out really nice, and it's easy to work with, where you don't get a lot of drips. It's the other things they need to be more concerned about. They need to apply the paint with the right tools, or they will have brush strokes, but typically, that's operator error, and it's from overworking it. That's easy enough to troubleshoot.

Susan: What is milk paint, for those of us who don't know?

Rachel: There's a lot of popular terminology in today's DIY painting world. There are chalk paints, milk paints, glazes, gel stains. Those are some popular words you come across. Milk paint is something that has been around for a very long time. Old school milk paint is a powder you mix and shake. General Finishes milk paint comes premixed and ready to use. It is a highly engineered acrylic-based paint that's made to stick to wood. Milk paint could be a little bit misleading, with regards to the General Finishes, but it is one of those popular terms that's out there now.

My Experience Using General Finishes Daily in My Business

Susan: Tell us about your experience with using General Finishes.

Rachel: I own a business named Restyle Junkie, in Phoenix, Arizona. We're licensed contractors, and the majority of our business is professionally painting clients' kitchen and bathroom cabinets, and we almost exclusively use General Finishes paint. Any time you use something every single day, I think it gives you the authority because you have had experience with it. I've worked with so many different types of cabinets, in so many different settings, homes, and situations, so it's really my experience with this particular product, on different surfaces, that has given me the education on what works and what doesn't work. I teach a popular class in Phoenix, at the shop. It's how to DIY your cabinets with General Finishes paint, and it's basically the exact same thing that I teach the people who work for me professionally doing clients' cabinets. We don't use a sprayer in our everyday work. We use certain products to de-gloss and sand our cabinets and prime them. We definitely use the General Finishes to paint and seal. When you not only use it every day, but you're teaching it, it gives you the knowledge of how to share that information with others.

Susan: If someone's interested in this class, can you tell us more about it?

Rachel: If they live in Phoenix, they can definitely come and take one of our DIY classes.

If the class times don't work for them, they can get a group of four or more and work with me to make their own custom class.

If they live out of state, or they've got too much going on to get into the shop, they can have access to the exact same information we guide our students through at **www.restylejunkiediy.com** and they can download some of my tutorials. They'll receive all the information that my students get in class, and I walk them through every single step of the way. They get to see my dog, Lola, which is a bonus. Honestly, you'll get everything, from the list of supplies that we use to where we purchase them.

Another place where people get into trouble is when they take down their cabinets and don't figure out a labeling system, so they can paint them, and then when they go to put them back up, it's a hot mess to figure out which cabinet goes where. In our class, we educate them on the way that we label, so when you go to reinstall cabinets, it's super easy, and you're not fighting with the person you're putting up and reapplying the cabinets with. We go over cleaning your cabinets and bases because there are lots of tips and tricks to that. Another topic in my class is taping and putting paper around your cabinets. You want to protect some of your surfaces and how to get clean lines between your wall and your cabinet. Of course, we go over applying paints and then applying clear coat, and lastly we go over re-installing, so that's the easy part for you. We hope that they'll take pictures of their cabinets. We hope they watch that video and share it with their social media because we're just as proud of you as you are of yourself.

Susan: Awesome. Where can they go for more information about this?

Rachel: If they're interested in the tutorials, they can go to **www.restylejunkiediy.com**. We also have a very active Facebook page, which is Restyle Junkie, and Instagram, as well, which is restyle.junkie.

Susan: If someone is in Phoenix, how can they work with you?

Rachel: If they'd like us to repaint their cabinets for them, we always welcome everyone to come into our shop. We are located across from the Deer Valley Airport in North Phoenix. We are open seven days a week. Our store number is **623-580-5222**. We have a showroom filled with color inspiration, and we have tons of cabinet samples of past work we've done and lots of pictures. We're also retailers of General Finishes paints, so if they're in the area, they can certainly come buy. We sell tons of paint by the gallon and can always special order whatever they need.

Susan: I want to thank you for explaining to us that, at the end of the day, it is just paint, and it can be fixed; however, with the right knowledge and the right product ahead of time, DIYers can literally add thousands of dollars' worth of value to their home and have the satisfaction of having done it themselves. I think that's brilliant.

Rachel: Absolutely. It doesn't have to be that hard. It's just knowing what products to use and how to apply them, and really not having to go research and navigate it yourself because it is overwhelming and can produce analysis paralysis.

Here's How to Use General Finishes Milk Paint to Get a Professional, Durable Finish for Your Kitchen and Bathroom Cabinets

You've seen what a difference new-looking cabinets can make in a kitchen. You've devoured DIY Pinterest boards, watched dozens of how-to tutorials, and read blogs from other DIYs on how to paint your cabinets yourself.

Yet you haven't gotten started because you are worried that if you make a mistake, it will look worse than when you started or start to peel after a short while. There is also conflicting information about what types of paint you should use. Do you need to prep your cabinets before painting, or can you skip that step, as some people suggest? Should you glaze? What about topcoat?

That's where I come in. I help people just like you learn how to use General Finishes paint to get a professional, durable finish for your kitchen and bathroom cabinets.

Here's three ways I can help you right now:

Option 1: If you live in the Phoenix, AZ area, attend one of my DIY classes. I walk you through each step of the DIY process in great detail, so you never have to wonder if you're doing it the right way. Get a group of four or more together, and create a custom class as well.

Option 2: If you live out of state, you can have access to the same exact material that I train my local clients in, including a full supply list of the tools I use to apply top coat that will protect your paint job without brush strokes and yellowing.

Option 3: Follow me on social media, where I show you before-and-after projects and share updated tips for getting a professional-looking result every time.

Most people know that you can add thousands of dollars in value to your home if you paint the build-grade, honey oak cabinets that a lot of homes have, but they are too afraid of ruining their kitchen by choosing the wrong type of paint or applying it poorly.

Now you can stop spending so much time on research and take the guesswork out of painting your cabinets by using General Finishes milk paints. Now you can paint with confidence.

If you'd like my help, just go to **www.restylejunkiediy.com** and sign up for one of my upcoming classes or tutorial series.

www.ingramcontent.com/pod-product-compliance
Lightning Source LLC
Chambersburg PA
CBHW060552030426
42337CB00019B/3524